FANTASTIC FACTS ABOUT

THE ANCIENT WORLD

Authors
Anita Ganeri, Hazel Mary Martell, Brian Williams

Editor
Jane Walker

Design
First Edition

Image Co-ordination
Ian Paulyn

Production Assistant
Rachel Jones

Index
Jane Parker

Editorial Director
Paula Borton

Design Director
Clare Sleven

Publishing Director
Jim Miles

This is a Parragon Book
First published in 2000
Parragon, Queen Street House, 4 Queen Street, Bath, BA1 1HE, UK

Parragon has previously printed this material in 1999 as part of the Factfinder series

2 4 6 8 10 9 7 5 3 1

Produced by Miles Kelly Publishing Ltd
Bardfield Centre, Great Bardfield, Essex CM7 4SL

ISBN 0-75253-383-5

Printed in Italy Milanostampa Caleppio Milano

FANTASTIC FACTS ABOUT

THE ANCIENT WORLD

p

CONTENTS

INTRODUCTION

No-one knows for certain, but it seems the first human-like creatures appeared around 4 million years ago. Thousands of years later, a huge change in lifestyle occurred when people began to domesticate animals, grow crops and live in permanent settlements. Find out about some of the civilizations of the ancient world – Mesopotamia, Egypt, Greece, Rome and India, and how these early cultures have left their mark on the world.

ANCIENT WORLD is a handy reference guide in the *Fascinating Facts* series. Each book has been specially compiled with a collection of stunning illustrations and photographs which bring the subject to life. Hundreds of facts and figures are presented in a variety of interesting ways and time-bars provide information at-a-glance. This unique combination is fun and easy to use and makes learning a pleasure.

THE ANCIENT WORLD

4 million years ago to AD 500

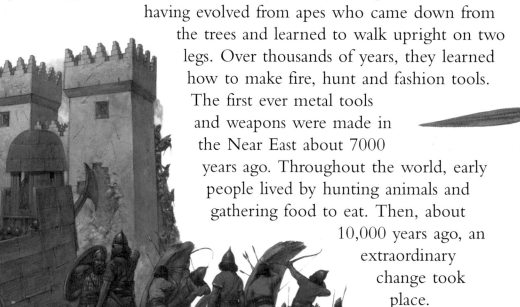

The period from about 4 million years ago to
AD 500 covers a vast sweep of the world's history,
from the appearance of the first human beings to
the fall of the Roman empire. Our earliest ancestors
appeared in Africa some 2.5 million years ago,
having evolved from apes who came down from
the trees and learned to walk upright on two
legs. Over thousands of years, they learned
how to make fire, hunt and fashion tools.
The first ever metal tools
and weapons were made in
the Near East about 7000
years ago. Throughout the world, early
people lived by hunting animals and
gathering food to eat. Then, about
10,000 years ago, an
extraordinary
change took
place.

People learned how to grow crops and raise their own animals, rather than hunting and gathering. They began to build permanent homes, followed by towns and cities. By about 5000 BC, the world's first civilizations began to emerge along rivers where the land was rich for farming – Sumerians, Assyrians, Babylonians, then the ancient Egyptians, Greeks and Romans. Civilizations flourished too in India, China, Persia and in North and South America.

9

THE FIRST HUMANS

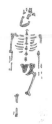

The first human-like creatures appeared on our planet about 4 million years ago, in Africa. These 'man-apes' came down from the trees, and began to walk on two legs. The most complete man-ape skeleton was found in Ethiopia, East Africa, in 1974. Its scientific name was *Australopithecus* (meaning southern ape), but the skeleton was nicknamed 'Lucy'. The first true human beings, called *Homo habilis,* or 'handy man', appeared about 2.5 million years ago. A million years

FROM APE TO HUMAN
Early people gradually became less like apes and more like humans.

Southern ape

Handy man

Upright man

Neanderthal man

Modern man

The hand axe was one of the earliest tools ever made. It was invented by Homo erectus *around 2 million years ago. Modern humans used hand axes until about 13,000 BC.*

later another species, *Homo erectus,* or 'upright man', appeared.

Early humans, or hominids, had bigger brains and were more intelligent than the man-apes. They learned to make tools, to hunt and gather food, to make shelters and fire and to communicate. Modern humans, *Homo sapiens sapiens,* our direct ancestors, first lived about 100,000 years ago. By about 40,000 BC, they had spread across Europe and had reached Australia.

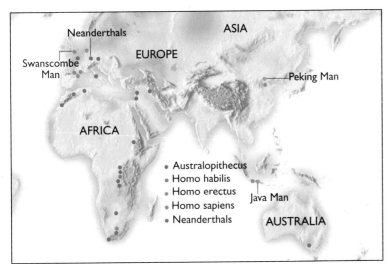

This map shows where important fossil remains of early people have been found.

c. 4 million years BC
Australopithecus appear in Africa. They walk on two legs instead of on all fours.

c. 2.5–2 million years BC
Homo habilis (handy man) appear in Africa. They are the first people to make tools.

c. 1.5 million years BC
Homo erectus (upright man) appear in Africa. They were the first people to learn how to use fire.

c. 120,000 BC Neanderthal man appears in Africa, Asia and Europe. They are the first humans to bury their dead.

c. 40,000 BC *Homo sapiens sapiens* (modern man) is now living in many parts of the world, including Australia.

c. 13,000 BC Modern humans cross from Asia into the Americas for the first time.

TOOLS AND ART

The first known tools were made from pebbles more than 2 million years ago. Gradually tools became more advanced. People soon discovered that flint was one of the best tool-making materials. It was very hard, and it could be chipped into different shapes and sizes. Early people shaped flints into tools such as sharp-edged hand axes, knives, blades, scrapers, choppers and needles. Stone Age weapons included harpoons and sharp spearheads and arrowheads. These were made from flints, bones and antlers. Bows and arrows, the earliest shooting weapons, were first used about 15,000 years ago.

PREPARING A HIDE

Stone Age people used stone blades to skin the animals they killed and scrape the hides clean. When the blade edges became blunt, they could easily be resharpened by chipping. The prepared hides were used for making clothes, tents and bags.

Antler spearhead

Flint scraper

Flint fire lighter

Stone lamp and grinder

Antler burin

Bone shuttle

Pieces of hide were sewn together using needles made of antler or bone.

Peg holds skin.

CAVE ART

Some 40,000 years ago artists painted pictures of the animals they hunted on the walls of their cave shelters. Cave paintings have been found in Europe, Africa, Asia and Australia. The most famous paintings in Europe are in the Lascaux Caves in southern France.

This bison painting was found in the Altamira Caves in Spain. It dates from about 12,000 BC.

Knife blade to cut skin.

c. 2 million years–10,000 BC The Old Stone Age. First stone tools.

c. 40,000 BC Rock engravings in Australia.

c. 24,000 BC Cave paintings in Namibia, Africa.

c. 17,000 BC Cave paintings in France and Spain.

From c. 10,000 BC The Middle Stone Age. A greater variety of stone tools.

From c. 8000 BC The New Stone Age. Stone tools, such as sickles and hoes.

c. 5000 BC The Copper Age. People make metal tools and weapons for the very first time.

c. 3000 BC The Bronze Age begins in the Near East. Bronze is an alloy, or mixture, of copper and tin.

c. 1000 BC The Iron Age begins in Europe.

13

LIFE IN THE ICE AGES

About 24,000 years ago, temperatures across the world plummeted and the Earth was gripped by freezing, icy weather. A huge sheet of ice, more than 200 m thick in places, covered about a third of the Earth's surface. This is what we call the "Ice Age" – the last glacial period, which ended about 10,000 years ago. Experts think that ice ages are caused by changes in the path taken by the Earth as it orbits the Sun. Even the slightest difference can drastically affect the amount of heat reaching the Earth.

As the seas froze over during the Ice Age, sea levels fell by over 100 m in some places, exposing bridges of land between the continents. The Bering Strait between Siberia and Alaska became dry land, creating a bridge

between Asia and North America up to 1000 km wide. The first people to reach North America probably walked across this land bridge. Conditions were extremely harsh for the people who lived near the ice sheets. Woolly mammoths were a valuable source of meat, skins for clothes and bones for weapons and carvings, but mammoth hunting was tough, dangerous work. The men hunted in groups, driving the mammoth into a corner or up against a cliff. Then they closed in for the kill, attacking the mammoth with sharp spears made of flint and wood and large stones. One mammoth could provide enough meat to feed a group for many months.

c. **2 million** BC The Quaternary ice age begins.

c. **22,000** BC The Ice Age enters its latest glacial. Ice covers about a third of the Earth.

c. **16,000** BC The last Ice Age reaches its coldest point. People living at Mezhirich in the Ukraine build huts from mammoth bones.

c. **13,000** BC Hunter-gatherers cross from Asia into North America via the now exposed Bering Strait.

c. **12,000** BC The Bering Strait floods over again, as the ice starts to melt and sea level rises.

c. **10,000** BC In Europe, the glaciers begin to retreat and the Ice Age ends.

c. **6000** BC Rising sea level separates Britain from the continent of Europe.

THE FIRST FARMERS

About 10,000 years ago, people learned how to grow crops and to rear animals for their meat, milk and skins. Instead of finding food by hunting wild animals and gathering nuts, berries and roots, people found they could grow enough food on a small patch of land. They began to settle in one place and build permanent homes. They were the first farmers.

EARLY FARM LIFE

Life on a farm in Europe around 3000 BC was hard work. Farmers dug the ground with deer antlers. They planted seeds from wild plants and harvested the crops with stone sickles.

Farmers started to build permanent homes.

Stone axes were used to fell trees and clear ground.

The harvested grain was ground into flour for bread.

Clay storage pots

Kiln

CROPS AND FARM ANIMALS

Plants and animals that are grown or raised by people are known as domesticated. Wheat and barley were two of the first crops grown by farmers. These first domesticated plants were grown from seeds collected from wild plants. The crop was harvested and the grain used to make bread and beer. Farmers also learned how to tame and breed wild animals. The first domesticated animals were sheep, goats and pigs.

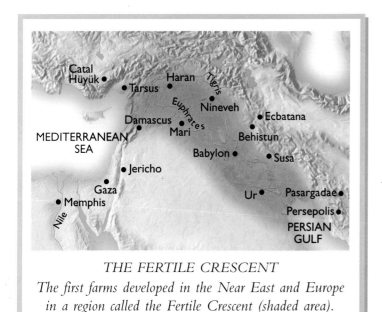

THE FERTILE CRESCENT
The first farms developed in the Near East and Europe in a region called the Fertile Crescent (shaded area). Many farming settlements became important towns.

c. 10,500 BC The first clay pots are made in Japan.

c. 8000 BC Farming begins in the Near East and in Southeast Asia. Sheep are domesticated in Iraq.

c. 7000 BC Farming develops in Central and South America.

c. 7000 BC Clay pots are made in the Near East and Africa to store grain and water.

c. 6500 BC The oldest known textiles are woven in Turkey.

c. 5000 BC Farming begins in China, Egypt and India, and spreads to Europe.

c. 4400 BC Horses are domesticated in Eastern Europe and used for riding for the first time.

c. 4000 BC The first ploughs are used in the Near East. They are made of sharply pointed, forked sticks.

THE FIRST TOWNS

As the world's population increased, towns grew up with a more complex way of life. Trade grew between the towns, as neighbouring farmers bought and sold their surplus produce. The ruins of two ancient towns have provided archaeologists with a fascinating glimpse into the past – Jericho in Jordan, and Çatal Hüyük in Turkey. People have lived in the town of Jericho continuously since about 8000 BC to the present day. Its massive stone walls have been destroyed many times – not by invading enemies but by a series of earthquakes.

RUINS OF HISHAM'S PALACE
Hisham's Palace, in Jericho, was a royal hunting lodge. It was built in the 8th century AD but was never completed.

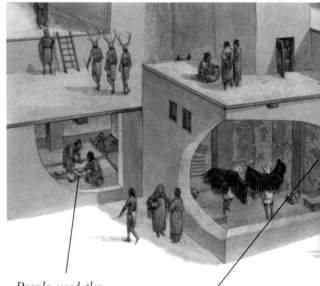

A FLOURISHING TOWN
The buildings in the Turkish town of Çatal Hüyük around 6000 BC included houses and workshops. Others seem to have been religious shrines. For safety, people lived in interconnecting, rectangular houses, with no doors. The rooftops acted as streets.

People used the rooftops as streets.

Wall paintings depicted vultures and headless men.

ÇATAL HÜYÜK, TURKEY

Built on a fertile river plain, the town of Çatal Hüyük was a successful farming settlement. Its wealth was also based on cattle-breeding and trade in obsidian (for making tools and weapons). By 6500 BC, Çatal Hüyük was flourishing and some 5000 people lived there.

Walls were decorated with plaster models and statuettes.

Long wooden ladders to reach rooftops.

c. 9000 BC A shrine stands on the site of ancient Jericho in the Near East.

c. 8000 BC Jericho grows into a thriving town of some 2000 people. It is one of the oldest known towns, built on the west bank of the river Jordan. The first bricks are made by Jericho's people.

c. 7000 BC Jericho is destroyed by an earthquake, but the town is later rebuilt. The Turkish town of Çatal Hüyük is founded. Its people are successful farmers and traders.

c. 6500 BC The oldest known textiles are made in Çatal Hüyük. They are linen, made from the fibres of the flax plant, and sewn into clothes.

MESOPOTAMIA AND SUMER

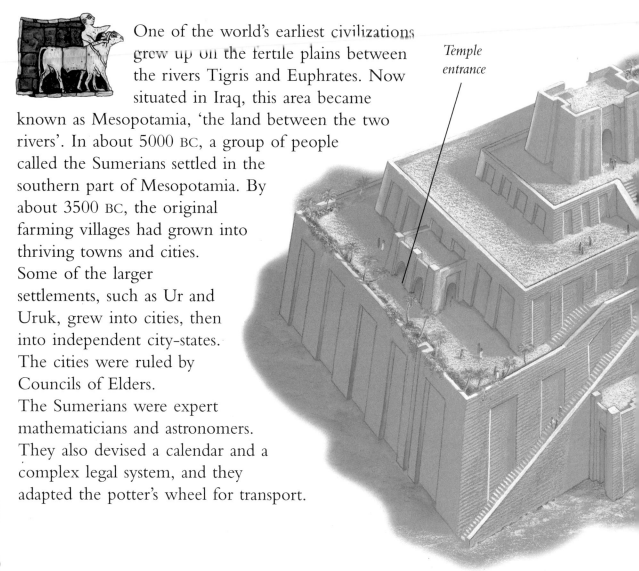

One of the world's earliest civilizations grew up on the fertile plains between the rivers Tigris and Euphrates. Now situated in Iraq, this area became known as Mesopotamia, 'the land between the two rivers'. In about 5000 BC, a group of people called the Sumerians settled in the southern part of Mesopotamia. By about 3500 BC, the original farming villages had grown into thriving towns and cities. Some of the larger settlements, such as Ur and Uruk, grew into cities, then into independent city-states. The cities were ruled by Councils of Elders. The Sumerians were expert mathematicians and astronomers. They also devised a calendar and a complex legal system, and they adapted the potter's wheel for transport.

Temple entrance

Their most important breakthrough, however, was the invention of a system of writing, known as cuneiform, in about 3500 BC.

THE ZIGGURAT AT UR
This great ziggurat, or stepped temple, was built in Ur in about 2100 BC. It was worshipped as the home of the Moon god, Nanna.

Platform

Main stairway

MAGNIFICENT JEWELS
This Sumerian woman's jewellery is made from gold and silver. The jewellery is inlaid with precious stones, such as lapis lazuli.

- **c. 5000 BC** Early Sumerians begin to farm in Ubaid, southern Mesopotamia (Iraq).
- **c. 4000 BC** The Sumerians learn how to smelt metal and use sailing boats on the Tigris and Euphrates rivers.
- **c. 3500 BC** The Sumerians invent writing and the wheel. They discover how to make bronze from copper and tin.
- **c. 2900–2400 BC** Kings are established in the main Sumerian cities.
- **c. 2400–2100 BC** Sumer is conquered by the Akkadians, then by the Gutians.
- **c. 2100 BC** The city of Ur reaches the height of its power under King Ur-Nammu.
- **c. 2000 BC** Ur is destroyed by the Elamites. The Sumerian civilization comes to an end.

21

ANCIENT EGYPT

The first villages of ancient Egypt were established some 7000 years ago. In time, these small settlements formed two kingdoms – Lower Egypt in the delta of the river Nile and Upper Egypt along the river valley. In about 3100 BC, King Menes, the ruler of Upper Egypt, united the two kingdoms and built his capital at Memphis. He established the first dynasty (line of kings) of ancient Egypt.

THE PYRAMIDS
The pyramids were built as tombs for the early pharaohs. They housed the pharaoh's body and priceless treasures to accompany him into the next world. The Great Pyramid of Giza was built for King Khufu some 4600 years ago.

Capstone

An outer coating of white casing blocks covered the whole pyramid.

Limestone blocks

QUEEN NEFERTITI
Nefertiti was the chief wife of King Akhenaten who ruled Egypt from about 1364 BC to 1347 BC.

POWERFUL PHARAOHS

The king was the most powerful person in ancient Egyptian society and every aspect of Egyptian life was under his control. From about 1554 BC, the king was given the honorary title of pharaoh. Two officials, called viziers, helped him govern and collect taxes. The country was divided into 42 districts, each governed on the pharaoh's behalf by officials called nomarchs. Further officials were put in charge of the major state departments such as the Treasury.

- **c. 5000–3100 BC** Nile valley cultures appear.
- **c. 4000 BC** Boats on the Nile begin to use sails.
- **c. 3200 BC** Early hieroglyphs are used in Egypt.
- **c. 3100 BC** King Menes unites Lower and Upper Egypt.
- **c. 3100–2686 BC** Archaic Period.
- **c. 2686–2150 BC** The Old Kingdom. The first pyramids are built.
- **c. 2580 BC** The Sphinx and Great Pyramid at Giza are built.
- **c. 2150–2040 BC** First Intermediate Period.
- **c. 2040–1640 BC** The Middle Kingdom. King Mentuhotep II reunites Egypt and restores order.
- **c. 1640–1552 BC** The Second Intermediate Period (Dynasties 14 to 17). The Hyksos people from Asia overrun Egypt.

23

EGYPTIAN BELIEFS

The ancient Egyptians believed firmly in life after death. When a person died, their soul was thought to travel to an underworld, called Duat. Here the soul had to pass a series of ordeals in order to progress to a better life in the next world.

For a person's soul to prosper in the next world, their body had to survive intact. The ancient Egyptians discovered how to preserve bodies by using the process of mummification. After the internal organs had been removed, the body was dried out, oiled and wrapped in linen strips, then placed in its coffin. Animals were preserved in this way, too.

CANOPIC JARS
When a body was mummified, the dead person's internal organs (liver, lungs, stomach and intestines) were removed. They were carefully wrapped and stored in four containers called canopic jars. The jars were placed in a chest inside the tomb.

Jar stopper

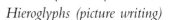
Hieroglyphs (picture writing)

THE KINGDOM OF THE GODS

The pharaoh's body was taken to his tomb in a decorated funeral barge. A proper burial ensured a place in Osiris' kingdom.

Osiris Amun Isis Horus

THE VALLEY OF THE KINGS

The kings of the New Kingdom were buried in tombs cut deep into a valley near Thebes, called the Valley of the Kings. This was meant to deter the tomb-robbers who had stripped the pyramid tombs bare.

Unfortunately, most of these tombs were ransacked too.

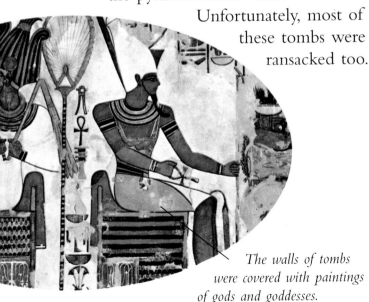

The walls of tombs were covered with paintings of gods and goddesses.

c. 1552–1085 BC The New Kingdom in Egypt (Dynasties 18 to 20).

c. 1479–1425 BC Reign of King Tuthmosis III. The Egyptian empire is at the height of its power.

c. 1347–1337 BC Reign of King Tutankhamun.

c. 1085–664 BC Third Intermediate Period (Dynasties 21 to 25).

c. 664–332 BC The Late Period (Dynasties 26 to 30).

c. 525–404 BC The Persians invade Egypt and rule as Dynasty 27.

332 BC Alexander the Great (founder of Alexandria) takes control of Egypt.

323 BC Alexander dies. Egypt is ruled by the Ptolemies.

30 BC Cleopatra, the last of the Ptolemies, commits suicide. Egypt becomes a province of the Roman empire.

25

THE INDUS VALLEY

Around 3000 BC, another great early civilization grew up along the banks of the river Indus in ancient India (present-day Pakistan). Called the Indus Valley civilization, by 2500 BC it had reached the height of its power. Its two great centres were the cities of Harappa and Mohenjo Daro, each with a population of some 40,000 people. From about 2000 BC, however, this mighty civilization began to decline. This may have been caused by flooding, by a change in the course of the Indus or by over-grazing of the land.

Streets were laid out in a grid-like pattern.

The houses of mud brick had bathrooms and a drainage system.

The Great Bath

A TRADING CIVILIZATION

The Indus Valley civilization had a highly organized system of trade. Merchants traded grain and other agricultural produce, grown on the fertile river plains, as well as artefacts made by the cities' artists and craft workers. Goods were traded for precious metals and cloth.

MOHENJO DARO

Like other cities in the Indus valley, Mohenjo Daro was laid out on a grid pattern. Each city had a citadel, with important buildings, such as the Great Bath, used for religious rituals.

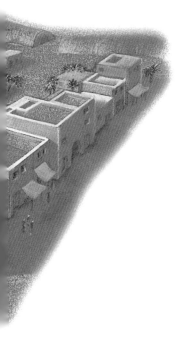

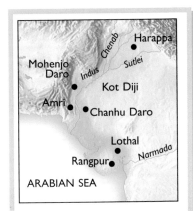

This map shows the extent and main cities of the Indus Valley civilization. This region now lies inside modern-day Pakistan.

c. 3000 BC Farming settlements grow up along the valley of the river Indus in northwest India (now Pakistan).

c. 2500 BC The Indus Valley civilization is at its height.

c. 2000 BC Some Indus sites start to show signs of decline.

c. 1500 BC The region is taken over by the Aryans, groups of Indo-Europeans from Iran. Their religious beliefs mix with those of the Indus cities to form the basis of the Hindu religion, which is still practised in India today.

MEGALITHIC EUROPE

From about 4500 BC, people in Europe began building monuments of massive, standing stones, called megaliths. These were placed in circles, or upright next to one another, with another stone laid horizontally on top.

Stone circles were laid out according to strict mathematical rules, but no one is sure what they were for. They may have been observatories for studying the Sun, Moon and stars, or temples for religious ceremonies. Experts also think that both human and animal sacrifices may have taken place inside the circles.

STONEHENGE, ENGLAND
The most famous stone circle is Stonehenge in England. Built from about 2800 BC, the stones were positioned to align precisely with the rays of the Sun on Midsummer's Day.

The largest stones form a horseshoe shape within the outer circle.

Outer circle of stones

MONUMENTS TO THE DEAD

Megalithic builders constructed stone monuments over the graves of their dead. These were often long, passage-like chambers, lined with megaliths, and buried under a mound of earth, called a barrow. Offerings of food and drink were left at the entrance, for use in the next world.

Druid priest

Fallen stone

DRUID WORSHIP
Druids used Stonehenge for their religious ceremonies centuries after it was built.

c. 4500 BC People start building megaliths in western Europe.

c. 4000 BC First passage graves are built at Carnac, France.

c. 3200 BC Newgrange grave is built in Ireland.

c. 2800–2000 BC Stonehenge, England, is built. The monument was built in three stages.

c. 2750–2000 BC Megalithic temples are built on the island of Malta.

THE MINOANS OF CRETE

The Minoan civilization was the first major civilization in Europe. It began on the island of Crete and was named after its ruler, King Minos. It was at the height of its power from about 2000 BC. The Minoans had a rich and glittering culture, with a highly organized society and flourishing economy. Minoan merchants travelled throughout the Mediterranean, trading wine, grain and olive oil, produced on the island, for luxury goods, such as amber, ivory and precious metals.

THE PALACE OF
KNOSSOS
Knossos was the largest Minoan palace. The walls of the royal apartments were decorated with frescos, or wall paintings, which have provided valuable clues about Minoan life.

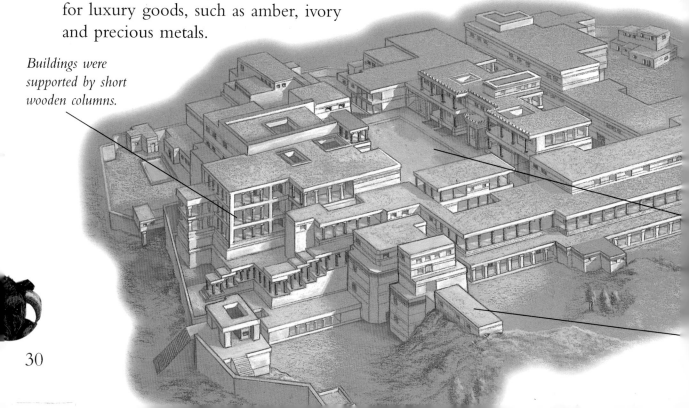

Buildings were supported by short wooden columns.

30

THE MINOTAUR
According to Greek legend, a terrible monster, half-man, half-bull, lived in a labyrinth (maze) under the palace of Knossos.

MINOAN PALACES

Each large Minoan town was built around a splendid palace, housing hundreds or even thousands of people. Palaces were royal residences as well as trading centres. They also contained shrines, workshops and living quarters for officials. By 1450 BC, however, most of the palaces had been destroyed, probably by earthquakes or volcanic eruptions, and Crete was taken over by the Mycenaeans.

The central courtyard was used for religious ceremonies.

c. 6000 BC The first farmers settle in Crete.

c. 3000–1000 BC People on Crete and mainland Greece learn how to make bronze.

c. 2000 BC The first palaces are built on Crete.

c. 1700 BC The palaces are destroyed by earthquakes and are later rebuilt.

c. 1600 BC The first Mycenaeans reach Crete.

c. 1450 BC A volcanic eruption destroys all the palaces on Crete, including Knossos.

c. 1100 BC The end of the Minoan civilization.

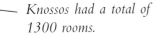

Knossos had a total of 1300 rooms.

31

THE MYCENAEANS

From about 1600 BC to 1100 BC the Mycenaeans dominated mainland Greece. They lived in separate, small kingdoms, although they shared the same language and beliefs and are named after their greatest city, Mycenae. Here evidence of their culture was first discovered. The Mycenaeans built their great palaces on hill tops, surrounded by massive stone walls. This type of fortified city was called an acropolis, which means 'high city' in Greek. These fortifications made their cities much easier to defend from attack.

MYSTERY OF THE MASK

This gold death mask was believed by Heinrich Schliemann to cover the face of Agamemnon, the legendary king of Mycenae. Modern scholars, however, think that the graves found by Schliemann date from about 300 years before Agamemnon's time.

THE TROJAN HORSE
According to legend, the Trojan War began when Mycenaean soldiers were smuggled into the city of Troy inside a huge wooden horse.

GOLDEN TREASURE

In 1876, the German archaeologist Heinrich Schliemann began excavating a circle of stone slabs inside the city walls of Mycenae. He discovered five shaft graves, sunk deep into the ground. They contained the bodies of 16 members of the Mycenaean royal family, five of whom had gold death masks covering their faces. Alongside lay a priceless hoard of golden treasure.

GATEWAY TO MYCENAE
The Lion Gate, the main gateway into Mycenae, was built in about 1250 BC. The two carved lions may have been symbols of the Mycenaean royal family.

c. 1600–1100 BC The Mycenaeans dominate mainland Greece.

c. 1450 BC The Mycenaeans become rulers of Crete.

c. 1250 BC The traditional date of the fall of Troy.

c. 1200 BC Mycenaean culture begins to decline, possibly due to crop failure and a weak economy. People begin to abandon the great cities.

c. 1100–800 BC The Dark Ages in Greece.

ANCIENT CHINA

The earliest civilizations in China grew up along the banks of three major rivers – the Chang Jiang (Yangtze), Xi Jiang (West River) and Huang He (Yellow River). From about 2205 BC, China was ruled by a series of dynasties (families). The Shang Dynasty ruled for more than 400 years before being conquered by the Zhou Dynasty. During the reign of the Zhou, many wars were fought between rival kingdoms, but it was also a period of economic growth and of trading success, with Chinese silk, precious jade and fine porcelain being traded abroad.

THE GREAT WALL OF CHINA
The Great Wall, built between 214 and 204 BC, formed a huge barrier more than 2250 km long, 9 m high and wide enough for chariots to drive along it.

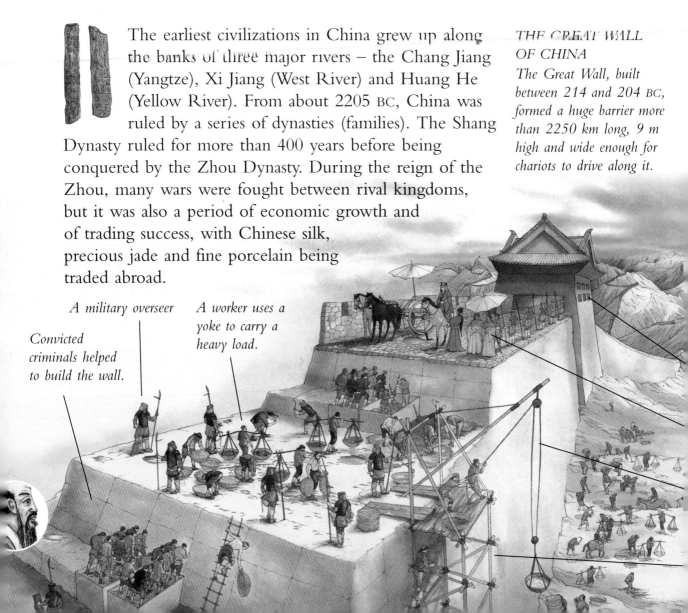

A military overseer

A worker uses a yoke to carry a heavy load.

Convicted criminals helped to build the wall.

CONFUCIUS
The prophet and philosopher Confucius dedicated himself to teaching people how to live in peace. His thoughts and teachings influenced many Chinese people.

THE QIN DYNASTY

Gradually, the war-like Qin (or Ch'in) Dynasty united the country and established the empire that gives China its name. The first emperor, Shi Huangdi, reorganized government and standardized money, weights and measures. The Qin built the Great Wall of China to keep out the hostile Hsung Nu people (the Huns), as well as an extensive road and canal network.

Watch tower

Nobles watched the building work.

Pulley to lift earth from works below.

Bamboo scaffold

c. 1766–1027 BC The Shang dynasty rules China.

1027–256 BC The Zhou dynasty rules China.

c. 551 BC Birth of the great teacher, Confucius.

481–221 BC The so-called Warring States Period when most of China is in civil war.

221 BC Shi Huangdi unites China and founds the Qin dynasty. He becomes China's first emperor.

212 BC Shi Huangdi burns books that contain different ideas from his own.

210 BC Death of Shi Huangdi. He was buried with a vast army of 10,000 life-sized clay soldiers.

202 BC Qin dynasty collapses and the Han dynasty rules China until AD 9.

EARLY WRITING

About 5500 years ago the Sumerians invented the first fully developed system of writing, called cuneiform. It represented words with symbols made up of wedge-shaped strokes (the name cuneiform means 'wedge-shaped'). These were impressed onto wet clay, using a reed pen, and the clay tablets were baked hard in the sun. The Sumerians used cuneiform to keep temple records and merchants' accounts. At about the same time, the ancient Egyptians were using a system of picture writing known as hieroglyphics. Each picture, or hieroglyph, stood for a picture or sound. Hieroglyphs were extremely complicated so highly trained scribes were employed to read and write them.

Cuneiform tablet

Hindu symbol 'Om' (the name of God).

PICTURE SYMBOLS

In the earliest writing systems, picture symbols were used to represent either words or individual characters. In some systems, such as the Chinese one, several thousand characters were in use. At first, these characters were drawn as picture symbols but they gradually became more abstract in form.

Arab numerals

This cave painting was made thousands of years before any proper system of writing was developed.

LETTERS AND NUMBERS

By about 1000 BC, the Phoenicians used a simple alphabet of 22 letters. A Greek version was adapted by the Romans for writing Latin (the basis of today's English alphabet). Numerals (1, 2, 3 etc.) were developed from a number system used by Hindus in India.

Phoenician alphabet

Hieroglyphic tablet

Chinese writing

     around 1500 BC

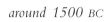   *before 213 BC*

    after AD 200

tree   moon   bird

- **c. 3500 BC** The Sumerians invent the cuneiform writing system.
- **c. 3500 BC** Hieroglyphs are used for the first time in Egypt.
- **c. 2500 BC** Merchants from the Indus Valley civilization use carved stone seals bearing a written inscription, possibly the merchant's name.
- **c. 1766–1027 BC** During the reign of China's Shang dynasty people predict the future using oracle bones decorated with early Chinese writing.
- **1027–256 BC** During the Zhou dynasty Chinese writing consists of several thousand characters.
- **c. 1000 BC** The Phoenician alphabet is well developed.
- **c. 727 BC** The Greeks adopt the Phoenician alphabet.

37

PHOENICIANS

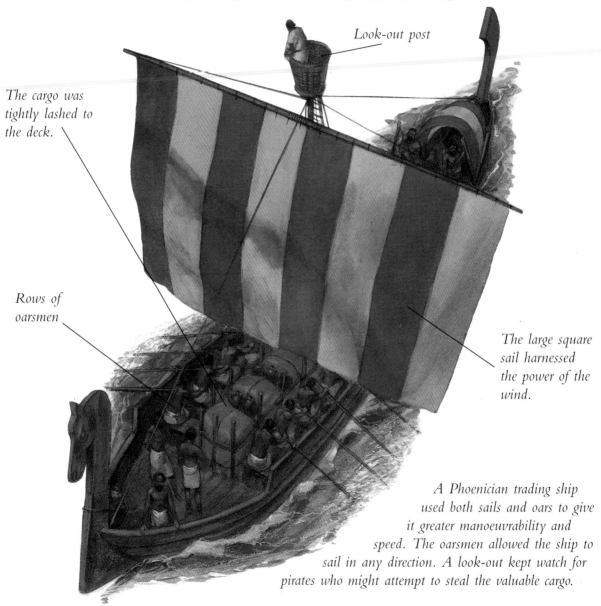

Look-out post

The cargo was
tightly lashed to
the deck.

Rows of
oarsmen

The large square
sail harnessed
the power of the
wind.

A Phoenician trading ship
used both sails and oars to give
it greater manoeuvrability and
speed. The oarsmen allowed the ship to
sail in any direction. A look-out kept watch for
pirates who might attempt to steal the valuable cargo.

The greatest traders and seafarers of the ancient world were the Phoenicians. They lived along the eastern coast of the Mediterranean (now part of Syria, Lebanon and Israel). Here, in about 1500 BC, they founded their greatest cities – Tyre, their main port, and Sidon. These became the flourishing centres of a vast trading network. The Phoenicians traded goods, such as glassware, timber, cedar oil, purple-dyed cloth and ivory throughout the Mediterranean, venturing as far west as Britain and down the African coast. In return they bought silver, copper and tin.

GREAT SEAFARERS

The Phoenicians had magnificent ships made of cedar wood – long, fast galleys for war and broader, sturdier ships for trade. They were also expert navigators, relying on the winds and stars to find their way.

TRADE ROUTES
This map shows the main trade routes and trading colonies of the Phoenicians.

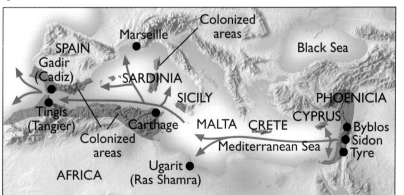

c. 1200 BC The beginning of the Phoenicians' rise to power.

c. 1200–350 BC The Phoenicians are the leading trading nation in the Mediterranean.

c. 1140 BC The Phoenician colony of Utica is founded in North Africa.

c. 1000 BC The Phoenician alphabet is well developed.

c. 814 BC The city of Carthage is founded in North Africa.

729 BC The Assyrian king, Shalmaneser V, invades Phoenicia.

c. 727 BC The Greeks adopt the Phoenician alphabet.

332 BC Alexander the Great conquers Phoenicia.

146 BC Rome defeats the Phoenician colony of Carthage at the end of the Punic Wars.

ANCIENT AMERICA

From about 1200 BC, two great civilizations grew up in ancient America – the Olmecs in western Mexico and the Chavin along the coast of northern Peru. Their ancestors had crossed the Bering Strait from Asia to America thousands of years before. The Olmec civilization began in about 1500 BC around the Gulf of Mexico. One of the main centres of Olmec culture was La Venta, whose people earned their living by fishing the rich waters and farming. The Olmecs were also skilled artists and craft workers, producing hundreds of sculptures and carvings from stone, jade and clay.

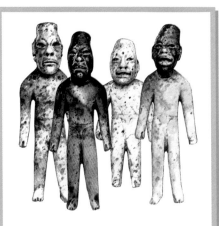

OLMEC CARVINGS
These tiny jade and serpentine figures were found at La Venta in 1955. They had been carefully buried with sand.

PYRAMID BUILDERS
The Olmecs built huge stepped pyramids made of earth. Here they worshipped their gods and performed religious ceremonies. The pyramid at La Venta was 34 m high. Around it lay several squares that were paved to look like jaguar masks.

THE CHAVIN CIVILIZATION

The Chavin civilization, which is named after Chavin de Huantar in the Andes Mountains, began in Peru in about 1200 BC and lasted for about 1000 years. Chavin de Huantar was a religious centre, with a huge temple surrounded by a maze of rooms and passageways.

c. **1200–300 BC** The Olmec civilization flourishes on the coast of western Mexico.

c. **1200–200 BC** The Chavin civilization flourishes on the coast of northern Peru.

c. **1100 BC** Olmecs build a great ceremonial centre at San Lorenzo.

c. **1000 BC** Olmec city of La Venta becomes a major centre for fishing, farming and trade.

c. **850–200 BC** Chavin de Huantar in the Peruvian Andes is at the height of its power.

c. **700 BC** Olmecs abandon San Lorenzo.

c. **400–300 BC** La Venta is abandoned and destroyed.

ASSYRIANS

In about 2000 BC, the Assyrians gained their independence from their powerful neighbours in Sumer and Akkad. They established a line of warrior-kings, under whose leadership they conquered a mighty empire, which was at its greatest during the New Assyrian empire (around 1000–612 BC). The Assyrians were tough, fearless soldiers. They ruled by force and showed no mercy.

Shield

Iron-tipped battering ram

Archer

HITTITE WARRIORS
The Hittites were a war-like people from Anatolia (in modern-day Turkey). They were the first to use chariots for warfare.

'KINGS OF THE UNIVERSE'

The Assyrian kings believed that they had been chosen to rule by the gods and so represented the gods on Earth. They were given grand titles such as 'King of the Universe'. The king was head of the government and army, and he was also responsible for the temples and priests. To display their wealth and power, kings built magnificent cities and palaces. Palace walls were decorated with carved reliefs of conquests as well as showing scenes from everyday life.

Assault tower

UNDER ATTACK

The Assyrian army used fearsome assault towers mounted on wheels to breach (break through) the city walls of their enemies. The towers had iron-tipped battering rams that could be swung to either side to smash through walls and doors.

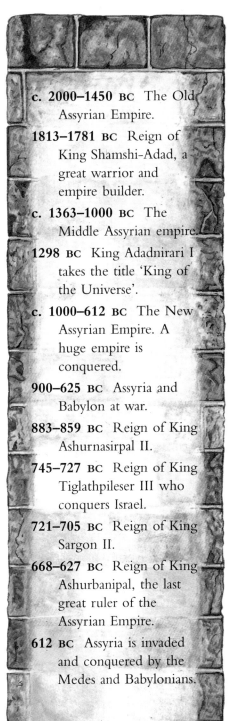

c. 2000–1450 BC The Old Assyrian Empire.

1813–1781 BC Reign of King Shamshi-Adad, a great warrior and empire builder.

c. 1363–1000 BC The Middle Assyrian empire.

1298 BC King Adadnirari I takes the title 'King of the Universe'.

c. 1000–612 BC The New Assyrian Empire. A huge empire is conquered.

900–625 BC Assyria and Babylon at war.

883–859 BC Reign of King Ashurnasirpal II.

745–727 BC Reign of King Tiglathpileser III who conquers Israel.

721–705 BC Reign of King Sargon II.

668–627 BC Reign of King Ashurbanipal, the last great ruler of the Assyrian Empire.

612 BC Assyria is invaded and conquered by the Medes and Babylonians.

BABYLONIANS

Babylon first grew powerful under the rule of King Hammurabi (c. 1792–1750 BC). He conquered the other kingdoms in Mesopotamia and extended Babylon's frontiers, making the city of Babylon capital of his new empire.
Hammurabi's code of law is the oldest surviving in the world. After his death, Babylon declined in power and was invaded by the Hittites, Kassites, Chaldeans and Assyrians. In the 6th century BC, King Nebuchadnezzar II conquered a huge empire and Babylon regained its former glory. The Persians captured the kingdom in 539 BC.

The gardens were planted with exotic flowers and trees.

Upper terrace

THE HANGING GARDENS OF BABYLON
One of the Seven Wonders of the ancient world, the Hanging Gardens were built during the reign of Nebuchadnezzar II. According to legend, his Persian wife missed the green hills of her homeland and so created her own terraced gardens.

THE CITY OF BABYLON

Situated on the banks of the river Euphrates (in modern Iraq), Babylon was a major trading centre. It was also a flourishing religious complex, especially for the worship of the god Marduk, patron of the city. Nebuchadnezzar II rebuilt Babylon in magnificent style.

Water was taken from the Euphrates to water the gardens.

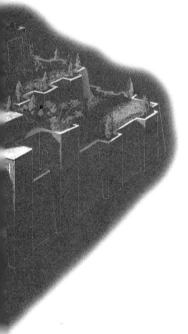

Lower terrace

THE GRANDEST GATE
One of eight massive city gates, the Ishtar Gate marked Babylon's northern entrance. It was named after the goddess of love and war.

c. 1894 BC The Amorite people establish Babylon in Mesopotamia.

c. 1792–1750 BC Reign of King Hammurabi. Babylon rises to power.

c. 1595 BC Babylon is invaded by the Hittites, then the Kassites.

c. 1595–1155 BC The Kassites rule Babylon.

c. 1126–1105 BC Reign of King Nebuchadnezzar I.

c. 731–626 BC Assyrians and Chaldeans fight for control of Babylon.

c. 626–529 BC The new Babylonian Empire re-emerges as a major power in the Near East.

c. 626–605 BC Reign of King Nabopolassar.

c. 605–562 BC Reign of Nebuchadnezzar II.

586 BC Nebuchadnezzar destroys Jerusalem and exiles its people to Babylon.

c. 539 BC The Persians conquer Babylon.

45

ANCIENT GREECE

By about 800 BC, Greece saw the rise
of a new civilization whose influence
has lasted to the present day.
Ancient Greece was divided into
independent city-states, the two
most important being Athens and
Sparta. Most city-states were ruled by
wealthy nobles and later, following
revolts, by absolute rulers called
tyrants. In about 508 BC, a new
type of government called
democracy was
introduced in Athens.
It gave every male
citizen a say in the running of the
city. When the Persians invaded Greece
in 490 BC, the city-states joined
forces and defeated the
invaders.

Bronze helmet

*A heavy round
shield protected the
soldier's body.*

*Split skirt-like
tunic*

Leg armour

IN BATTLE

*A hoplite, or foot soldier, was the
most important part of the Greek
army. Greek hoplites formed a
phalanx – a block of soldiers eight
or more rows deep.*

BATTLE SHIPS
Greek warships had sails and several banks of oars on either side, which made them very fast and easy to manoeuvre.

DEFEAT BY SPARTA

Greece's newly won security did not last long and, in 431 BC, war broke out between Athens and Sparta. The Peloponnesian Wars lasted for 27 years and tore the country apart. The Spartans besieged Athens and the city finally surrendered in 404 BC.

c. 900 BC State of Sparta founded by the Dorians.

c. 800–500 BC The Archaic Period. Greece revives after The Dark Ages, a period of decline.

776 BC The first Olympic Games are held.

c. 500–336 BC Greek culture reaches its height in the Classical Period.

490–449 BC The Persian Wars. Greece wins.

479–431 BC Athens prospers.

447–438 BC The Parthenon is built in Athens.

431–404 BC The Peloponnesian Wars between Athens and Sparta. Sparta wins.

371 BC Sparta is defeated by Thebes.

338 BC The Macedonians defeat the Greeks.

336–30 BC The Hellenistic Period.

147–146 BC Greece becomes part of the Roman Empire.

GREEK CULTURE

Greek civilization came to an end over 2000 years ago, yet its influence on politics, philosophy, art and architecture, language and literature can still be felt today. Much of our language and many of our ideas about science and art come from the ancient Greeks, who were great scholars, thinkers and teachers. At first, they answered questions about life and nature with stories about the gods. Later, they started to look for more practical, more scientific ways of understanding the world about them.

Circular area for acting.

The actors (all male) wore masks.

The audience sat on stone seats arranged in rows.

THE OLYMPIC GAMES

Sport in ancient Greece was not only a means of entertainment, but also a way of keeping men fit and healthy for fighting. The oldest and most famous competition for athletes was the Olympic Games, held every four years at Olympia, in honour of Zeus. Athletes trained hard for many months before the games.

EVERYDAY LIFE
Much of our knowledge about the ancient Greeks comes from vases and vessels. They were decorated with scenes from daily life showing what the Greeks wore, how they lived and so on.

GREEK THEATRE

Drama played a very important part in the lives of the ancient Greeks. At first, plays were performed in the market place. Later, open-air theatres like this one were built across Greece. The largest could hold an audience of 18,000 people.

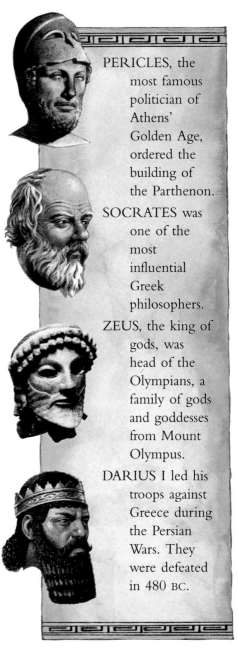

PERICLES, the most famous politician of Athens' Golden Age, ordered the building of the Parthenon.

SOCRATES was one of the most influential Greek philosophers.

ZEUS, the king of gods, was head of the Olympians, a family of gods and goddesses from Mount Olympus.

DARIUS I led his troops against Greece during the Persian Wars. They were defeated in 480 BC.

49

ALEXANDER THE GREAT

While the city-states of Greece were in disarray following the Peloponnesian Wars, the new power of Macedonia took full advantage of the situation. When Philip II came to the throne in 359 BC, he transformed Macedonia into the greatest military force of the day. In 338 BC, at the battle of Chaeronea, Philip's army gained control of Greece, uniting the Greeks and Macedonians against the Persians. In 336 BC Philip was assassinated and the throne passed to his son, Alexander. Under Alexander's leadership, the Macedonian empire became the largest in the ancient world.

ALEXANDER'S EMPIRE
The map shows the extent of Alexander's empire and the routes of his campaigns. It took Alexander just 13 years to conquer a vast empire stretching from Greece eastwards to India.

A GREAT LEADER
Alexander was an even more brilliant leader and general than his father, Philip II. This is Alexander on his favourite horse, Bucephalus..

CONQUERING THE PERSIANS

Alexander conquered the Persians not only to acquire their lands but also to replenish his treasuries with their wealth. By 331 BC he was king of the whole of Persia. To strengthen ties with the Persians, Alexander wore Persian clothes and married a Persian princess.

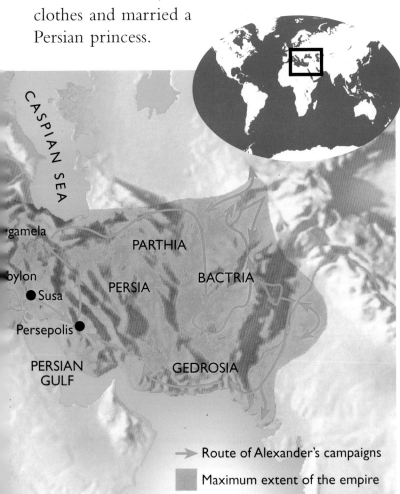

CASPIAN SEA

PARTHIA

BACTRIA

PERSIA

gamela

bylon

● Susa

Persepolis ●

PERSIAN GULF

GEDROSIA

→ Route of Alexander's campaigns

Maximum extent of the empire

359 BC Philip II becomes King of Macedonia.

356 BC Alexander is born.

338 BC At Chaeronea, Philip wins control of the Greek city-states.

336 BC Philip is murdered. Alexander becomes king at the age of 20.

333 BC Alexander defeats the Persians at the battle of Issus.

332 BC Alexander marches on and conquers Egypt.

331 BC Alexander defeats the Persians at the battle of Gaugamela. Darius is assassinated and Alexander becomes King of Persia.

324 BC Alexander's tired army mutinies in India.

323 BC Alexander dies of a fever in Babylon.

323–281 BC The empire is split into three – Persia, Egypt and Macedonia.

147–146 BC Macedonia becomes part of the Roman Empire.

THE CELTS

The Celts probably first lived in France and Austria from about 600 BC. Gradually, Celtic tribes spread across southern and western Europe, conquering the lands and settling in hill-forts and farms. Famed and feared for their bravery in battle, the Celts were great warriors and individual warriors often fought on their own. Wars frequently broke out between the rival Celtic tribes. This helped the Romans to defeat the Celts more easily than if they had been a unified and efficiently run military force. Following defeat, much of their territory was brought under Roman rule.

CELTIC CULTURE

The Celts were highly skilled metalsmiths, making beautifully decorated weapons and jewellery. They were gifted poets and musicians, passing down stories and history by word of mouth. The Celts worshipped many gods and goddesses, offering sacrifices in their honour. Religious ceremonies were performed by priests, called druids.

QUEEN BOUDICCA
In AD 60, Boudicca (or Boadicea), the queen of the Iceni tribe from East Anglia, led a revolt against the Romans in Britain.

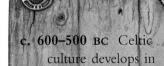

Animals kept in fenced area beside hut.

Timber framework.

A huge iron cooking cauldron hung over the fire in the centre of the hut.

Cloth made of woven wool.

LIFE IN A HILL-FORT

Safe within a hill-fort, each family lived with their animals in circular wooden huts with thatched roofs. The hill-forts were built on high ground to give a clear view of the surrounding countryside and of any intruders.

c. 600–500 BC Celtic culture develops in Austria and France.

c. 400 BC The Celts build farms and hill-forts in southern and western Europe.

390 BC The Gauls (French Celts) sack the city of Rome.

225 BC The Romans defeat the Gauls at the battle of Telamon in Italy.

58–50 BC Julius Caesar conquers all of Gaul (France).

52 BC Vercingetorix, a chieftain of the Arveni tribe in central Gaul, leads a revolt against the Romans. He is defeated by Caesar.

AD 61 Boudicca is defeated in a revolt she leads against the Romans in Britain.

THE ROMANS

Spear

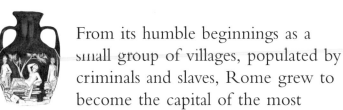

From its humble beginnings as a small group of villages, populated by criminals and slaves, Rome grew to become the capital of the most powerful empire the western world had ever seen. At first, Rome was ruled by kings, until about 509 BC when King Tarquin the Proud was expelled. For the next 500 years Rome became a republic. Power passed to the Senate, a law-making body made up of important nobles. It was headed by two elected officials, called consuls, who managed the affairs of the Senate and the Roman army.

THE ROMAN ARMY
Small units of Roman soldiers, called centuries, consisted of 80 men and were commanded by centurions. A soldier carried two basic weapons – a spear to throw as he neared the enemy, and a short sword for close combat.

Long shield

AN EMPIRE IS BORN

By about 50 BC, Rome had conquered most of the lands around the Mediterranean. However, rivalry between army generals and tensions between rich and poor plunged Rome into civil war. The republic crumbled, and in 27 BC Octavian, son of Julius Caesar, became the first Roman emperor.

ROMULUS AND REMUS

According to legend, Rome was founded by twin brothers called Romulus and Remus. They were rescued by a she-wolf after being abandoned.

753 BC The founding of Rome.

c. 509 BC The founding of the Roman Republic.

49 BC Julius Caesar is dictator of Rome.

27 BC The end of the Republic. Octavian is the first emperor.

AD 64 Fire devastates Rome.

c. AD 80 The Colosseum is completed in Rome.

AD 98–117 The empire is at its greatest extent.

AD 117–138 Hadrian rules.

AD 166–167 The empire is devastated by a plague.

AD 286 Diocletian divides the empire into west and east.

AD 391 Christianity becomes the official religion of the Roman Empire.

AD 410 Alaric the Goth sacks Rome.

AD 476 The last western emperor, Romulus Augustulus, is deposed.

ROMAN SOCIETY

The amazing expansion and success of the Roman empire was due largely to its army, the best trained and best equipped in the world. Soldiers were paid wages and joined up for 20 to 25 years. For many young men from good families, the army provided a stepping stone to a glittering political career. Ordinary soldiers were grouped into units, called legions, each made up of about 5000 men. The legions, in turn, were made up of smaller units, called centuries, of 80 men commanded by soldiers called centurions.

Augustus was the first emperor of Rome.

In 218 BC, during the Punic Wars, the Carthaginian general, Hannibal, led a surprise attack on the Romans by marching over the Alps with 35,000 men and 37 elephants.

Roman society was divided into citizens and non-citizens. There were three classes of citizens – patricians, the richest and most influential aristocrats; equites, the wealthy merchants, and plebians, the ordinary citizens, or 'commoners'. All citizens were allowed to vote in elections and to serve in the army. They were also allowed to wear togas. Non-citizens included provincials, people who lived outside Rome itself but in territory under Roman rule, and slaves. Slaves had no rights or status. They were owned by wealthy citizens, or by the government, and did all the hardest, dirtiest jobs.

AD **69–79** Vespasian rules the Roman empire.

AD **79–81** Titus rules.

c. AD **80** The Colosseum is completed in Rome.

AD **81–96** Domitian rules.

AD **96–98** Nerva rules.

AD **98–117** Trajan rules. The empire reaches its greatest extent.

AD **117–138** Hadrian rules.

AD **180** End of the *Pax Romana*, or Roman Peace, a time of stability in the empire.

AD **286** Emperor Diocletian divides the empire into west and east, each with its own emperor.

AD **391** Christianity becomes the official religion of the Roman empire.

AD **410** Sack of Rome by Alaric the Goth.

AD **451** Attila the Hun invades Gaul.

AD **476** The last western emperor, Romulus Augustulus, is deposed. The eastern empire continues as the Byzantine empire.

EMPIRES OF AFRICA

The first great African civilization, apart from ancient Egypt, grew up in Nubia (now in northern Sudan) around 2000 BC. It was the kingdom of Kush. In the 3rd century BC, the capital of Kush moved to Meroe, on the river Nile. The city became an important centre of iron-working. In western Africa (now in Nigeria), another iron-working centre developed in about 600 BC. These people, known as the Nok, mined iron and used it to make farming tools, arrowheads and spears.

A NOK VILLAGE

Life in a Nok village centred around farming and iron-working. The Nok smelted iron ore in a cylindrical pit furnace made of clay. This separated the metal from the rock. Potters used furnaces to fire their clay sculptures.

Goats provided milk and meat.

The people of Axum built stone obelisks. These huge towers may have been symbols of power or burial monuments for royalty.

THE KINGDOM OF AXUM

In northeast Africa (now in Ethiopia), the kingdom of Axum grew rich from buying and selling spices, incense and ivory. Its major trading partners were Arabia, Egypt and Persia. Although the people of Axum originally worshipped local gods, by the end of the 5th century AD most had become Christians.

Clay sculpture

From 2000 BC The kingdom of Kush begins in Nubia.

c. 900 BC Kush gains its independence from Egypt.

c. 600 BC The Nok culture begins in northern Nigeria.

c. AD 200 The Nok culture ends but has a lasting effect on the artistic styles of Africa.

2nd century AD The kingdom of Axum rises to power.

AD 320–350 King Ezana rules Axum and converts to Christianity.

c. AD 350 Axum overruns the city of Meroe and brings the Kushite kingdom to an end.

6th century AD Axum rules part of western Arabia.

c. AD 1000 The kingdom of Axum collapses as a new Islamic empire from Arabia expands.

59

EMPIRES OF INDIA

In about 321 BC, a young prince, Chandragupta Maurya, founded the first Indian empire stretching across northern India. Chandragupta's grandson, Ashoka, who came to the throne in 269 BC, extended the empire farther, until most of India came under Mauryan rule. Following a bloody battle against the people of Kalinga in eastern India, Ashoka was sickened by the killing and bloodshed. Filled with remorse, he converted to Buddhism and vowed from then onwards to follow its teachings of peace and non-violence. Ashoka travelled throughout his empire, listening to people's views and complaints.

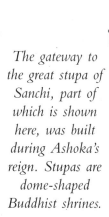

The gateway to the great stupa of Sanchi, part of which is shown here, was built during Ashoka's reign. Stupas are dome-shaped Buddhist shrines.

THE GUPTA EMPIRE

After the Mauryan empire collapsed, India was divided into several smaller states and kingdoms. The Guptas from the Ganges valley extended their power, ruling northern India for 200 years. Under Chandra Gupta II, India enjoyed a Golden Age. The arts flourished, and Hinduism became the main religion.

EMPEROR ASHOKA MAURYA

Ashoka, one of India's greatest rulers, has had a lasting effect on modern India. Its national emblem is copied from a pillar that Ashoka built, topped with four lions and four wheels.

c. 563 BC Buddha is born in Lumbini, Nepal.

c. 483 BC Buddha dies in Kushinagara, India.

c. 321 BC Chandragupta seizes power and founds the Mauryan dynasty.

269–232 BC Reign of Ashoka Maurya.

260 BC Ashoka converts to Buddhism after the battle of Kalinga.

c. 185 BC The Shunga Dynasty replaces the Mauryans.

c. AD 320 The beginnings of Gupta power emerges in the Ganges valley.

c. AD 350–550 The Gupta empire brings a Golden Age of Hinduism to India.

AD 380–415 The reign of Chandra Gupta II.

c. AD 550 Hun invasions weaken Gupta power. The empire splits into smaller kingdoms.

INDEX

ACKNOWLEDGEMENTS

The publishers wish to thank the following artists who have
contributed to this book.

Martin Camm, Richard Hook, Rob Jakeway, John James, Shane
Marsh, Roger Payne, Mark Peppé, Eric Rowe, Peter Sarson,
Roger Smith, Michael Welply and Michael White.

PHOTO CREDITS
Page 56 (BL) AKG London; page 32 (C) AKG London.

All other photographs from the Miles Kelly Archive.